ANIMALS AND THEIR YOUNG

How Animals Produce and Care for Their Babies

WRITTEN BY PAMELA HICKMAN

ILLUSTRATED BY PAT STEPHENS

Kids Can Press

My thanks once again to Pat Stephens for her lovely illustrations and to Marie Bartholomew for the design. A special thank you to my newest editor, Stacey Roderick, for keeping me on track while I've been living in the Caribbean.

For my nephew's new baby, Andrew James — PH

To the great people at Kids'N Us in Durham — PS

Kids Can Press acknowledges the financial support of the Ontario Arts Council, the Canada Council for the Arts and the Government of Canada, through the BPIDP, for our publishing activity.

Published in Canada by
Kids Can Press Ltd.
29 Birch Avenue
Toronto, ON M4V 1E2

Published in the U.S. by
Kids Can Press Ltd.
2250 Military Road
Tonawanda, NY 14150

www.kidscanpress.com

Edited by Stacey Roderick
Designed by Marie Bartholomew

Printed and bound in Hong Kong, China, by Book Art Inc., Toronto

The hardcover edition of this book is smyth sewn casebound.
The paperback edition of this book is limp sewn with a drawn-on cover.

CM 03 0 9 8 7 6 5 4 3 2 1
CM PA 03 0 9 8 7 6 5 4 3 2 1

National Library of Canada Cataloguing in Publication Data

Hickman, Pamela
    Animals and their young : how animals produce and care for their babies / written by Pamela Hickman ; illustrated by Pat Stephens.

Includes index.
ISBN 1-55337-061-9 (bound). ISBN 1-55337-062-7 (pbk.)

1. Parental behavior in animals — Juvenile literature. 2. Animals — Infancy — Juvenile literature. I. Stephens, Pat II. Title.

QL763.H52 2003   j591.56'3   C2002-902604-0

Kids Can Press is a /©rUs™ Entertainment company

Contents

Introduction

You may be an only child like a baby hippopotamus, or maybe you're a twin like most mountain goat kids. But imagine having to share your mother with 25 or more brothers and sisters all exactly the same age as you, the way a baby tenrec does! In this book you'll meet all kinds of animal families, big and small.

Most animals start life inside an egg, but where the eggs end up can be surprising. You'll discover mothers who carry their eggs around on their back and fathers who hatch eggs inside their mouth.

Instead of laying eggs, most mammals, such as dogs, cats and humans, give birth to live young. But what if your mother gave birth hanging upside down from a tree the way a sloth does? Bear mothers even sleep through the birth of their children!

Do you ever stay with a baby-sitter? Many animals leave their babies with other adults while they find food. Other baby animals are left all alone right from the start.

The life of a young animal may be very different from yours, or surprisingly similar. After reading this book, compare your parents with a puffin's, your childhood with a polar bear's and your education with an orangutan's. You may be amazed at what you discover!

Tenrecs

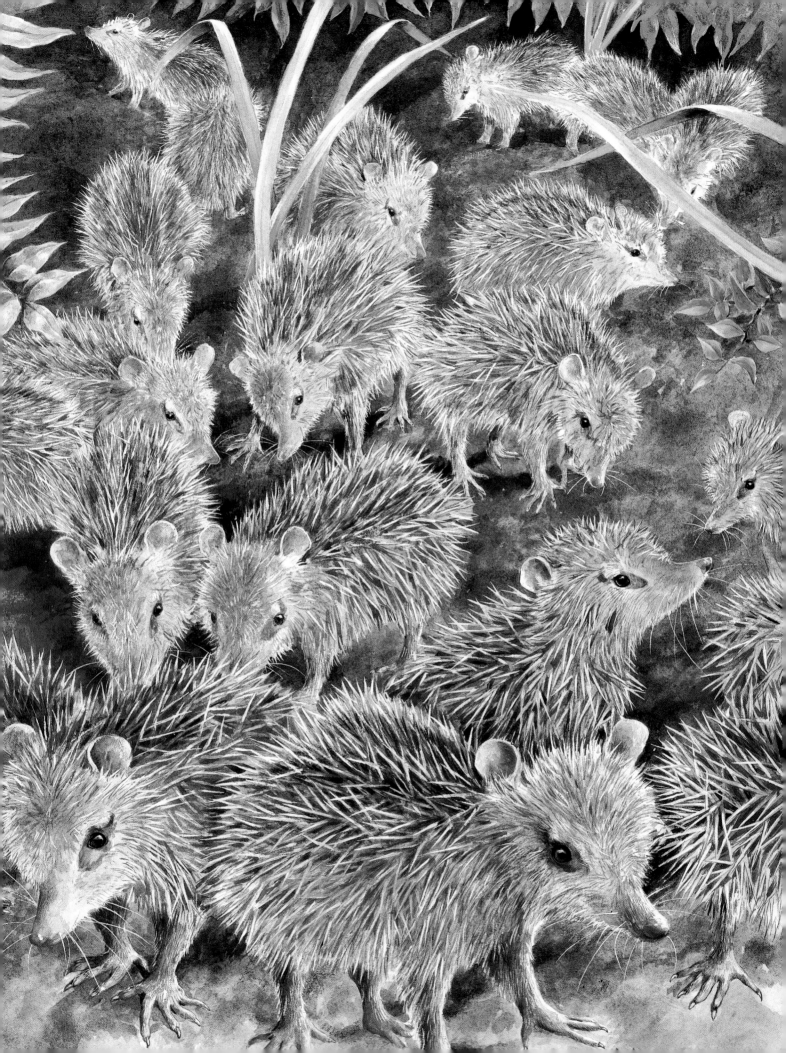

Starting out as an egg

Most baby creatures hatch from eggs. Frogs and fish lay soft, squishy eggs in the water. Reptiles, such as turtles, have leathery coverings on their eggs to keep them from drying out on land. Birds' eggs have the hardest shells of all.

Keeping eggs safe sometimes means hiding them, defending the nest or carrying eggs around until they are ready to hatch. Read on to discover some amazing egg protectors, such as these puffin parents who share the job of incubating their egg, or keeping it warm, for about a month and a half before it hatches.

If you were an Atlantic puffin chick ...

- you would be an only child.
- you would be covered with fine down feathers when you hatched in your burrow, or underground nest.
- you would be kept warm by a parent for the first week.
- you would be left alone while your parents went out fishing for your food.
- your parents would leave you after 40 days.
- you would fly to the sea one night and only return to land to nest several years later.

Eggs up close

Eggs come in an amazing assortment of sizes, colors and shapes, depending on the creature that has laid them. Insects lay the tiniest and most numerous eggs. They are so well hidden, often among plants, that most people never notice them. To see the soft, jelly-covered eggs of toads and frogs, you'd have to visit a pond or marsh. Finding a reptile's leathery eggs is also hard. Turtles lay their Ping-Pong ball-like eggs in holes dug in the ground, and snakes lay their eggs inside rotting logs or under rocks.

If you've ever watched birds nesting, you may have seen their eggs or found the empty shells on the ground below the nest. Most bird eggs are less than 5 cm (2 in.) long, but the extinct elephant bird's egg was bigger than this page.

Now the largest egg is laid by the world's biggest bird, the ostrich. Its eggs measure up to 18 cm (7 in.) long. The smallest bird eggs are the pea-sized eggs of hummingbirds. But no matter the size, each bird's egg is basically the same on the inside.

Hummingbird egg

Ostrich egg

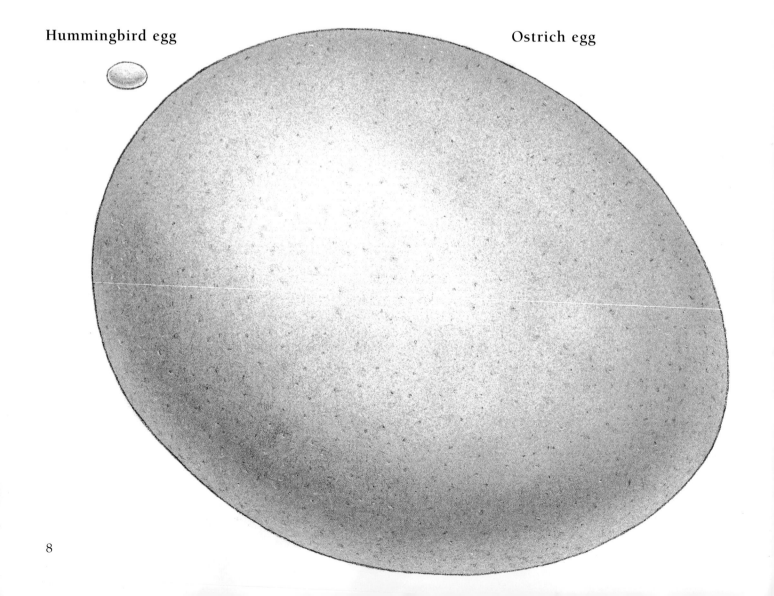

Inside an egg

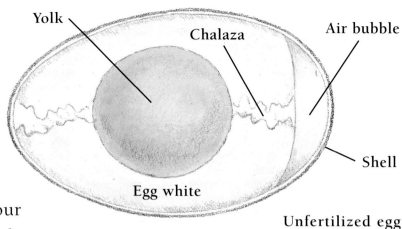

Yolk · Chalaza · Air bubble · Shell · Egg white

Unfertilized egg

You're probably most familiar with chicken eggs from the grocery store. Using this illustration as a guide, you can see the parts of an egg by cracking one open.

Before cracking the eggshell, put your thumb on the larger end of the egg and your index finger on the pointy end. Now press your fingers together as hard as you can. You will not be able to break the egg. The hard shell of a bird's egg is made of calcium carbonate crystals that are formed inside the mother's body. The way these crystals are arranged makes the eggshell very strong.

Inside the egg you will find a clear liquid, called the egg white. This provides water and cushioning for the embryo, or undeveloped baby. The yellow yolk provides food for the growing baby bird.

At each end of the yolk there is a thick white cord, called the chalaza, that connects the yolk to the eggshell. Just before the baby bird hatches, it breaks the air bubble in the wide end of the egg and takes its first breath of air. Then the baby uses a knob on its beak, called an egg tooth, to break through the shell.

The eggs you buy at the store have not been fertilized by a male bird, so there are no embryos inside. When an egg is fertilized, the growing embryo is attached to the yolk by a narrow stem.

Nests within nests

Some birds use guards to keep their eggs safe. An Australian warbler protects its eggs and young by building its nest beside a hornet's nest. The stinging hornets keep predators away but don't bother the birds. A kingfisher in Borneo goes one step further by laying its eggs right inside a bee's nest!

Eggs on the move

Once birds, turtles and snakes have laid their eggs, they can't pick them up or carry them away if danger threatens. The best they can do is to defend or hide the eggs from predators. Some other creatures, though, have incredible ways of safely carrying their eggs until they hatch. Check out the egg minders on these pages.

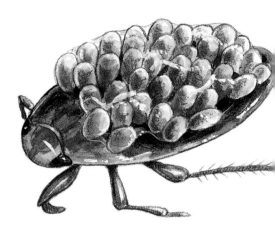

Once a female giant water bug lays her eggs, she sticks them to the male's back and he carries them around in the water to keep them safe.

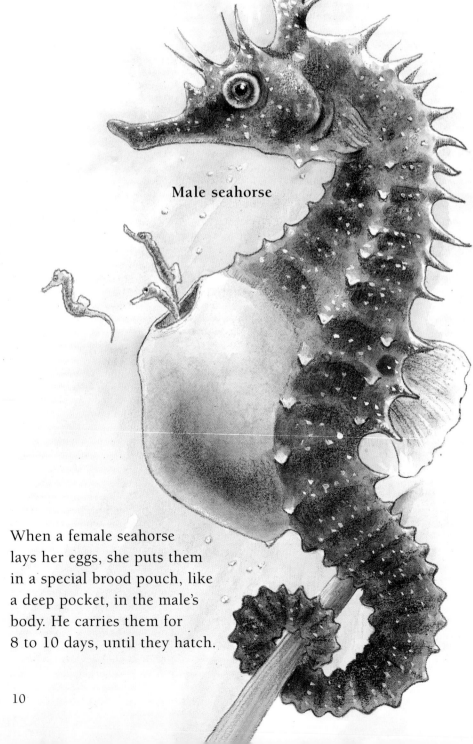

Male seahorse

When a female seahorse lays her eggs, she puts them in a special brood pouch, like a deep pocket, in the male's body. He carries them for 8 to 10 days, until they hatch.

Chile's tiny Rhinoderma frog starts life inside its father's vocal sac! The adult frog scoops the eggs into his mouth and stores them in his large throat pouch until they hatch and grow into froglets. When the froglets are old enough, the male opens his mouth and the young jump out.

Male Rhinoderma frog and froglet

Female Gastrotheca frog

After this Gastrotheca frog from South America lays her eggs, she transfers them to a pouch on her back. When the eggs hatch, the tadpoles grow and move under her skin until they can swim away through a slit in the pouch.

Female tarantula

A female tarantula wraps her eggs in a silky sac that she has spun and carries under her body until hatching day.

Eggs inside

Some eggs are never laid. Female sharks, rays and some snakes and fish are ovoviviparous. This means they keep their eggs inside their bodies. The young feed on the yolk and grow inside the eggs until they hatch inside their mother's body as smaller versions of the adults. The female then gives birth to live young.

Meet a monotreme

You know that birds come from eggs, but did you know that a few mammals do, too? The platypus and the spiny anteater, also called an echidna, are the only two egg-laying mammals in the world. They are in a special group of mammals called monotremes. Unlike other mammals, monotremes lay eggs, do not have nipples and do not have a regular body temperature.

Echidna

The platypus lives in the rivers of eastern Australia. The female lays two or three leathery eggs in a burrow and incubates them until they hatch about 10 days later.

Newly hatched platypuses are blind and helpless. Their mother has special glands on her belly that ooze milk, and the babies feed by sucking the milk off her hair. After six weeks the babies are furry, their eyes are open and they can leave the burrow for short swims. They are weaned, or stop drinking their mother's milk, at four to five months. Then they catch their own insects, frogs and crayfish for food.

First platypus discovered!

Over two hundred years ago, scientists were shocked by the remains of a strange creature from Australia. After examining the animal's large flat beak, hairy body and webbed feet, many thought it was a fake. Later, when a whole specimen was delivered, they had to agree that it was a real animal and called it a platypus.

Because of its hairy body, the platypus was considered a mammal. Locals in Australia told researchers that the animal laid eggs, but no one believed them, since at that time it was thought that all mammals gave birth to live young. Nearly one hundred years later a platypus was seen laying eggs, and scientists were finally convinced that an egg-laying mammal really did exist.

Platypuses

Happy birthday

You are a mammal. Like most mammals, you were born live and did not hatch from an egg. Mammals are divided into three groups: monotremes, marsupials and placentals. Monotremes are the egg-laying mammals you read about on page 12. Marsupials, such as kangaroos and opossums, are born live, tiny and underdeveloped. But most mammals are placental like you and are born after fully developing inside their mother.

These placental polar bears are born while their mother is hibernating. She wakes up only long enough to lick them dry and then goes back to sleep for another two months or so, while the babies snuggle and feed on her milk.

If you were a polar bear cub ...

- you and your twin would be born in mid-winter inside a snowy den.
- you would be small, hairless and deaf at birth. Your eyes wouldn't open for six weeks.
- your mother would teach you to swim and hunt in the warmer weather.
- you would be carried on your mother's back when you were tired.
- you would stay with your mother for up to two years.

Marsupial moms

Marsupials are mammals that are born at a very early stage in their development and their bodies still have a lot of changing and growing to do. Marsupial babies continue their development after they are born, usually in their mother's pouch, a natural "pocket" on the female's belly. Kangaroos are probably the best-known marsupials, but there are over 150 different kinds, including marsupial mice and cats.

Baby kangaroo inside mother's pouch

Nipple

Koala kids

The teddy bear-like koala is one of Australia's favorite marsupials and is a protected species. Koalas usually give birth to only one baby every second year. When a mother koala is ready to give birth, she licks her pouch clean. Then she licks her fur to make a path to her pouch that her baby can follow after it's born.

A newborn koala is less than 2.5 cm (1 in.) long. It crawls up to its mother's belly and into her warm, safe pouch. Inside the pouch, the blind, hairless baby immediately latches on to a nipple to feed and doesn't let go for several weeks.

While it nurses on its mother's nutritious milk, the young koala grows quickly. Within a few months it can leave the pouch for short periods of time. At seven months, the baby is too large to fit into its mother's pouch so she carries it on her back until it's about a year old.

Koalas

17

Placental parents

When you hear the word "baby," what do you think of? Probably something small, cute and cuddly. Some babies don't fit that description at all. A newborn blue whale calf measures about 7 m (23 ft.) long and weighs as much as two pickup trucks!

Like most mammals, whales are placental, which means their babies develop fully inside the mother's body. To feed the developing baby, placental mammals have a special organ called a placenta that connects the baby to the mother's blood supply. Food flows from the placenta through an umbilical cord to the baby so it can stay inside its mother until it is ready to be born. That's nine months for people and almost two years for an elephant!

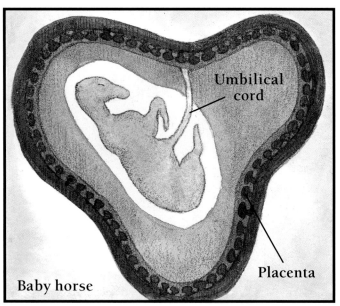

Umbilical cord

Placenta

Baby horse

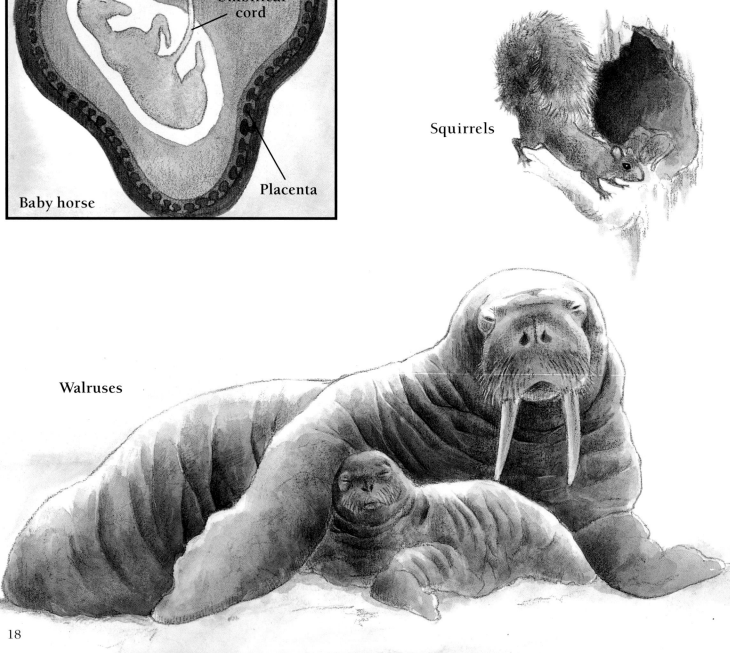

Squirrels

Walruses

Mice are born in soft, warm nests, but a baby giraffe starts its life off with a bump. Since its mother gives birth standing up, the baby drops 1.5 m (5 ft.) to the ground when it is born!

While most mammals are born on land, whales are born underwater, and walruses give birth on ice floes. Nest builders, such as some squirrels, mice and rats, have their babies high off the ground in trees or shrubs where they are safer from predators. Bat mothers give birth hanging upside down in caves or other shelters. Baby sloths are born while their mothers hang upside down from trees in the tropical forests of South America.

Four familiar faces

Quadruplets, or four babies born at once, are very rare for humans, but not for the nine-banded armadillo that lives in South America and the southern United States. It gives birth to identical quadruplets every time!

Giraffes

Sloths

19

Hardy or helpless?

Human babies are born helpless and need lots of care and protection for many years. Some wild animals, such as baby mice or blue jays, are also born defenseless. Others, like bison and ducklings, are hardier and can get up and go within hours.

A young animal's survival depends on a number of things, including food supply, parental care and how long it takes the animal to learn to feed and defend itself.

Some animals with many enemies, such as these rabbits, are helpless at birth, but they can look after themselves in only a few weeks.

If you were a cottontail kit ...

- you would be one of five or six in the litter.
- you would be small enough to fit on a child's hand.
- you would be blind, hairless and completely helpless at birth.
- your mother would cover your nest and leave you alone so she didn't attract predators. She would visit only to nurse you.
- you would grow quickly and leave your nest after five or six weeks.

How many and how often?

Humpback whales

Prey species also grow quickly to reproduce often and at an early age to make up for the young that die. A female Norway lemming can have a litter of seven babies every four weeks.

Norway lemmings

Have you ever heard the expression "multiplying like rabbits"? In one year, two pairs of rabbits can produce over 160 children and 3000 grandchildren!

If you are wondering why you don't see rabbits everywhere, it's because many of the babies are killed by predators. Animals that are prey to others tend to have large litters because many of their young don't survive. In contrast, the humpback whale has only one calf every one to three years. It has few predators and lives for many years.

Queen termite

The tenrec of Madagascar has the largest average litter for any placental mammal: over 25 at one time. But that seems very few compared with some egg-laying animals. A queen termite can produce thirty thousand eggs per day, and a female toad can lay twenty thousand eggs per season and a quarter million eggs in her life!

Toad

Baby boom or bust

Sometimes environmental
conditions such as food
supply and habitat affect
how many animals are born.
For instance, an Arctic fox
normally has a litter of 5
to 8 kits, but if lemmings
(their main food) are plentiful,
a fox may have 20 kits.

The loss of nesting habitat can
bring some species closer to extinction,
or dying out. If a piping plover, an endangered
species in Canada, can't find an undisturbed
beach, it will not nest. Similarly, if an
endangered sea turtle is disturbed while
coming ashore to lay her eggs, she will
return to the water without nesting.

Arctic foxes

Piping plover

Sea turtle

23

Protective parents

Wild animals are usually afraid of people and will leave if a person comes too close. But when a wild animal has young to protect, it may behave very differently. Some birds, such as swallows and terns, dive-bomb anyone who is too near their nest. A killdeer pretends it is injured to lure enemies away from its eggs or young. Large mammals, such as bears or moose, may attack if they sense that their young are in danger.

Parents of altricial, or helpless, babies often hide them in burrows, nests or thickets to avoid enemies. The altricial young of predators, such as bobcats, soon outgrow their hiding places, but they are still in danger of attack from other predators, such as owls or wolves. When bobcat kits are threatened, their parents defend them with their sharp claws and teeth. A black bear mother

Bobcats

teaches her cubs to quickly climb the nearest tree when in danger, while she stays to fight.

Even though precocial, or active, babies can get around soon after birth, they may still need their parents' protection. Giraffe parents use their sharp hooves to kick attackers and drive them off. Baby alligators are left alone, hidden in the plants growing along the water, while the mother goes off a little way to feed. She watches for danger, though, and quickly returns, bellowing and snapping her huge jaws if a predator approaches her young.

Animals that live in herds, such as caribou, often give birth all at once. When there are many babies in the herd, their chance of survival is better since predators can take only a few during an attack. By forming a protective circle around the calves, adult musk oxen defend the herd, pointing their large, horned heads out toward the enemy.

Musk oxen

In a flap

The Canada goose is a fierce defender of its nest. The male will hiss, peck, bite and raise its large wings, flapping them noisily to scare off potential nest robbers. Both parents defend their goslings, or young, often tucking them under their large wings for safety. The young geese stay with their parents for a year, flying south in the fall and returning with them to the northern breeding grounds the following spring.

Carry on

Imagine being carried in your mother's mouth, or hanging on to her hair while she moves from place to place. At birth, altricial babies cannot get around by themselves for several days or longer, so they must be carried if the adults want to move on. Even precocial babies get free rides sometimes, but some are just too big to carry. Fortunately, young giraffes, elephants, horses and whales can travel on their own soon after birth.

Baby animals hitch rides on their parents for all kinds of reasons. It helps them stay together, move quickly to find food and, most importantly, escape danger. Check out the pictures on these pages to see some of the ways animals carry their babies around. How would you like a ride in a crocodile's mouth?

Chimpanzees give their babies piggyback rides for up to five years!

Right after hatching, baby crocodiles are carried to water in a pouch in the bottom of their mother's mouth.

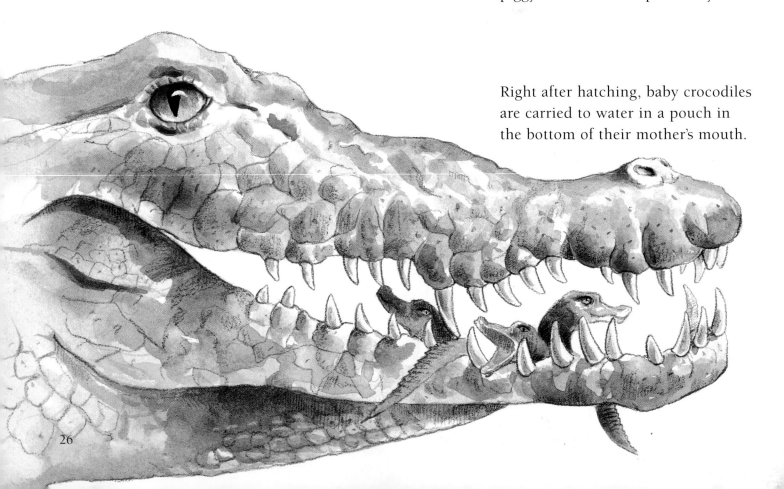

A sea otter pup is carried in the water on its mother's belly.

Baby loons get a free ride on their parent's back.

A young pangolin clings to its mother's tail to get around.

27

Who cares?

The amount of time a young animal spends with its parents depends on the species. A baby frog never sees its parents, but a young cougar stays with its mother for a year. A male elephant calf usually hangs around its mother until it's a teenager, but the females stay together for life.

A leatherback turtle will never know its mother. Once a female leatherback lays her eggs, she buries them in the sand. She hides the nest from predators by smoothing out the sand before heading back to the water. She nests, or lays eggs, several times in one breeding season but never comes back to see her babies hatch.

If you were a leatherback turtle baby ...

- the temperature in your nest would determine whether you were male or female.
- you would hatch in an underground nest on a tropical beach and spend four days digging your way out.
- you would head straight to the ocean and swim away.
- you would spend your first year mainly hiding from predators.
- you would never return to land if you were male. If you were female, you wouldn't return to nest for 10 to 15 years.

Home alone

You would never leave a newborn human baby alone and defenseless, but that is nature's way for many egg-laying animals, including most insects,

Mason wasp

fish and many reptiles and amphibians. How do they survive alone? The female's instinct, or natural behavior, is to protect her eggs by laying them in a safe spot. As well, insect eggs are often placed on plants that are food for the growing young. The mason wasp actually builds a little room for each egg and stuffs in a paralyzed caterpillar for the wasp larva to feed on when it hatches. In fact, earwigs are one of the few insects that stay around and care for their young after they hatch.

Earwig

Although most fish eggs are laid in the water and left to take care of themselves, angelfish and sticklebacks are two types of fish that stay and protect their eggs and young until the babies can survive on their own.

Stickleback

Angelfish

Most mammals are attentive parents, but a gray seal mother nurses her young for only three weeks on the breeding beach. Then she leaves the baby seal to molt, learn to swim and hunt on its own.

Gray seal

Alone or abandoned?

What should you do if you find a wild baby animal all alone? Probably the best thing would be to do nothing. Baby birds have to leave the nest when it gets too crowded, even if they can't fly. The parents are usually still nearby, taking care of their young, even if you can't see them. A wild baby mammal, such as a rabbit or fawn, may look abandoned but the adults often leave the young hidden while they find food. Hide nearby and wait a few hours. If the animal's parent doesn't return, you may need to offer care yourself. First keep the young animal warm and calm. Then call an animal care expert, the local wildlife or conservation officer or a local wildlife rehabilitation organization, if there is one in your area.

Young long-eared owl

Animal child care

Many children are looked after by baby-sitters or day-care workers while their parents work. Some wild animal babies are also watched over by caregivers other than their parents. Thousands of bats give birth at the same time in nursery caves where, later, the young are left with other adults while their parents go out to feed. Wolves, whales and giraffes also share the responsibility of looking after the young in their group. Sometimes the caregivers are family members. Often, two lion sisters share the care for their cubs, and baby elephants are watched over by various aunts in their herd.

Some birds also share the task of raising their young. King penguin parents leave their baby in the care of other adult penguins for two to three weeks at a time while they go looking for food.

Anis have communal nests, which means that several females lay eggs in one large nest. The adult birds

Ostriches

32

take turns incubating the eggs and feeding the hatchlings. Ostriches also have shared nests and form crèches, or nurseries, of up to one hundred chicks that are supervised by a few parents. By sharing the protection of the eggs and young, the adult birds can safely leave to find food and keep a lookout for danger.

And then there are cowbirds and cuckoos, who lay their eggs in the nests of other species of birds. Their young are "adopted" by the other parents and are fed and protected until they are old enough to look after themselves. Unfortunately, the natural babies in the nest are sometimes killed by the intruding birds.

Ani

A bushy tale

How do you look after a helpless, orphaned baby gray squirrel? Dr. John Paling of England slowly introduced an abandoned baby squirrel to a mother cat and her new litter of kittens. Although the squirrel was smaller than the kittens and looked and smelled differently, it was soon adopted into the family. At four weeks old, the kittens and the squirrel played together during the day and cuddled in their basket at night. But when the squirrel began to chew on the furniture and bury nuts in the kitty litter, the doctor knew it was time to prepare it for life in the wild. After six weeks, the doctor and his cats watched as their "squitten" left for its new life.

Raising a family

In most bird and mammal families, parents are kept busy feeding, teaching and defending the family. Both red fox parents help raise their family, but for many animals, the mother is the main caregiver. Atlantic puffin or hippopotamus females that have only one young at a time may have less work than pheasant or hare mothers that have many young to watch over. But the young of mammals with small litters tend to stay with their parents longer, while they grow to adult size and learn special survival skills.

Precocial birds, such as ducks, can feed themselves shortly after hatching, but the parent of altricial birds, such as warblers, must make several hundred trips a day in and out of the nest to keep its babies fed. Feeding time is much easier for mother mammals like this hippopotamus since they produce their own baby food — milk.

If you were a hippopotamus calf ...

- you would be an only child.
- you would be born on land or in shallow water. You would weigh 23 to 55 kg (50 to 120 lbs.).
- you would nurse underwater, coming up to breathe every few seconds.
- you would rest on your mother's back when you were tired. She would leave you with other females while she went to feed.
- you would be weaned at eight months, but stay with your mother for about two years.

Baby food

All mammal mothers produce milk to feed their babies. It's filling and contains special nutrients to make babies strong and fight diseases. Not all milk is alike, though. Species that live in cold habitats, such as whales and reindeer, have a high fat and protein content in their milk. This helps the babies build up their body fat quickly to keep them warm. A gray whale calf can gain half a kilogram (a pound) per hour during its first year!

At first, a human baby may feed eight or so times a day, but a humpback whale nurses about forty times a day! When a baby mammal gets bigger and more independent, the mother weans it. Then it's time for different food — the mushier the better, since baby mammals can't digest solid foods and some don't have teeth yet. After being weaned, wolf and coyote pups are fed meat that their parents have chewed, predigested and then spit up for their young.

Coyotes

Albatrosses

All you can eat

Soon after an animal is weaned, it usually finds its own meals. Baby mice quickly learn to forage, or search, for seeds and roots, and baby apes learn to pick fruit from trees. But young predators, such as foxes and lions, rely on their parents for food for much longer while learning to hunt for themselves. You might expect an adult lion to always make sure its cubs have eaten a good meal, but in a lion family, the adults eat first. If there isn't enough food for everyone, the cubs go hungry.

Seafood soup

Baby seabirds, such as albatrosses, also eat mushy food. After the first few weeks of a young albatross's life, both parents leave their single baby for up to 10 days at a time. They return with a load of squid and fish that they have already swallowed and predigested. Each parent spits up the soupy seafood, and the hungry chick gobbles it up. The parents continue feeding their baby for up to nine months, until it is able to go hunting on its own. Other than seabirds, most baby birds eat insects caught by their parents, even if they are seed eaters as adults.

Lions

37

Work and play

Often young animals learn by watching and copying adults. Baby birds learn to fly by watching their parents, and baby grizzly bears learn to fish the same way. A baby orangutan clings to its mother's fur for its first five years and learns everything it needs to know about survival by watching her.

Polar bears

Orangutans

Grizzlies

Some lessons are learned by playing games. Adult foxes bring live mice and voles home for their youngsters to chase and catch before eating. This helps the kits recognize prey and improves their hunting skills. Mother moose and mountain goats teach the male calves to fight by playing a head-butting game.

Animals also learn skills by playing with other youngsters of the same species, sometimes their brothers and sisters. Musk oxen calves play King of the Castle. One calf climbs a high piece of ground and the other calves try to butt it off. Young polar bears wrestle, chase each other and play Follow-the-Leader. These games build their muscles, make them quicker and better at self-defense and sharpen their hunting skills.

Sometimes young animals seem to play games just for fun, the way you and your friends do. River otters plunge down mudslides, and whales push and toss seashells and seaweed to each other. Dolphins are famous for jumping and splashing in front of boats. Beluga whales are known for another game: One whale dives to the bottom of the ocean and comes up balancing a rock on its head. The object of the game is for another whale to knock the rock off.

Moose

Index